Recipes by: Stephanie Fletcher

Photography: Phil Calvin

Arrangements: Stephanie Fletcher and Phil Calvin

Editing: Nicholas D'Acre

Copyright information:

BAKING
WITH BISCUIT

Biscuit's Chocolate Chippers

<u>Recipe</u>: (Makes 2 dozen)

INGREDIENTS:

2 c. flour

1/2 tsp. baking soda

3/4 c. Kerrygold salted butter, softened

1 c. light brown sugar

1/2 c. granulated sugar

1 egg

1 egg yolk

1- 10 oz. bag mini chocolate chips

DIRECTIONS:

1. In a stand mixer or with a hand mixer, combine butter, sugars, egg and egg yolk.

2. Sift flour and baking soda into wet ingredients. Mix until combined. Stir in by hand, chocolate chips.

3. With a 1 1/2 cookie scoop, put dough 2 inches apart on parchment lined cookies sheet.

4. Preheat oven to 325°, bake for 8-10 minutes. Should appear under cooked. Remove and let cool. Transfer to baking rack to cool completely.

COOKIES & CREAM COOKIES

<u>Recipe</u>: (Makes 12-15 cookies)

INGREDIENTS:

2 1/4 c. flour

1 tsp. baking soda

1 c. butter, softened

1/2 c. sugar

1- 3 oz. pkg. cookies and cream pudding

2 eggs

1 tsp. vanilla

Oreo cookies

White chocolate chips

DIRECTIONS:

1. In a stand mixer or using a hand mixer, in a large bowl combine all ingredients, mix until well combined.

2. Using a 1 1/2 cookie scoop, place dough 2 inches a part on a parchment lined cookie sheet. Preheat oven to 350°. Bake for 10 minutes.

3. Remove cookie sheet from oven and let cool 5-10 minutes. Place cookies on cooling rack until completely cooled.

Macadamia Cookies

Recipe : (Makes 2 dozen)

INGREDIENTS:

2 3/4 c. flour

1 c. light brown sugar

1/2 c. granulated sugar

1 c. butter, softened

1 1/4 c. macadamia nuts, crushed

2 eggs

1 tsp. vanilla

DIRECTIONS:

1. Beat butter, brown sugar, sugar and vanilla together in a medium bowl. Add eggs one at a time until well combined.

2. Mix flour in 1 cup at a time until well combined.

3. Fold macadamia nuts in.

4. Preheat oven to 350°, using a 1 1/2 cookie scoop place dough on parchment lined cookie sheet about 2 inches apart.

5. Bake at 350°, for 8-10 minutes. Remove from oven and cool 5-10 minutes. Transfer to cooling rack. Let cool completely.

MEXICAN WEDDING COOKIES

Recipe : (Makes 2 dozen)

INGREDIENTS:

1 c. pecans, crushed

1 c. butter, softened

2 c. powdered sugar

2 c. flour

2 tsp. vanilla

DIRECTIONS:

1. Beat butter, 1/2 c. powder sugar, flour, and vanilla in a mixing bowl, until well combined.

2. Chill in refrigerator for 2-4 hours, remove and fold in crushed pecans

3. Preheat oven to 350°, using a 1 1/2 cookie scoop, put dough out on parchment lined cookie sheet. Bake at 350° for 12-15 minutes.

4. Remove from oven and let cool, 5-10 minutes. Transfer to cooling rack. When cooled completely, roll cookies in remaining powder sugar.

Peanut Butter Cookies

Recipe: (Makes 2 dozen)

INGREDIENTS:

3/4 c. peanut butter

1/4 c. shortening

1 egg

1 can condensed milk

1 tsp. vanilla

1 1/2 c. flour

2 tsp. baking powder

DIRECTIONS:

1. Combine all ingredients in a stand mixer or in a medium bowl with a hand mixer.

2. With a 1 1/2 cookie scoop, put dough 2 inches apart on parchment lined cookies sheet. Place a criss-cross with a fork end on each dough ball.

3. Preheat oven to 350°, bake for 8-10 minutes. Remove and let cool, transfer to baking rack.

Pumpkin Chocolate Chip Cookies

Recipe: (Makes 2 dozen)

INGREDIENTS:

1 c. pumpkin puree

1 c. sugar

1/2 c. shortening

1 egg

2 c. flour

2 tsp. baking powder

2 tsp. cinnamon

1 tsp. baking soda

1 tsp. milk

1 tbsp. vanilla

3/4 c. chocolate chips

DIRECTIONS:

1. In a medium bowl whisk together pumpkin, sugar, shortening, and egg until well combined.

2. In a separate bowl, combine flour, baking powder and cinnamon.

3. Dissolve baking soda in milk and mix together until well combined. Stir into pumpkin mixture.

4. Add flour mix into wet ingredients and combine thoroughly.

5. Add vanilla and chocolate chips and fold into dough.

6. Preheat oven to 350°. Using a 1 1/2 cookie scoop, place dough balls on parchment lined cookie sheets. Bake at 350° for 9-11 minutes. Remove from oven and let cool 5 minutes. Place on cooling rack and let cool completely. Repeat until all dough is used.

BISCUIT'S BEST CHEESECAKE

Recipe: (Makes 1- 10 inch cheesecake)

INGREDIENTS:

Crust

2 1/2 lbs. cream cheese, room temperature

2 c. Graham crackers, crumbed

1 3/4 c. granulated sugar

1/2 c. butter, melted

2 tbsp. granulated sugar

3 tbsp. flour

5 eggs

2 egg yolks

1/4 c. heavy whipping cream

DIRECTIONS:

1. Place graham crackers, melted butter and sugar in medium bowl mix until crumbs are well coated and crumbly. Press into bottom and sides of 10 inch spring form pan. Bake at 350° for 10 minutes. Remove, let cool.

2. In a stand mixer, beat cream cheese, sugar, eggs, egg yolks and flour until super creamy. Fold heavy cream into cream cheese mixture with a spatula. Pour into spring form pan with crust.

3. Bake at 350° for 42 minutes, times may vary depending on your oven. Remove and let cool. Refrigerate once cooled, until served.

Chewy Brownies

Recipe: (Makes 1 8x8 pan)

INGREDIENTS:

3/4 c. cocoa powder

1 1/3 c. flour

1/2 tsp. baking soda

2/3 c. butter, melted

1/2 c. boiling water

2 c. granulated sugar

2 eggs

1 tsp. vanilla

Optional ingredients:

Nuts

Chocolate chips

DIRECTIONS:

1. Combine all ingredients, except boiling water in a medium bowl, mix until well combined. Add boiling water and stir slowly until incorporated.

2. Pour batter into greased 8x8 pan. Preheat oven to 350°. Bake for approximately 35-40 minutes, until tooth pick comes clean.

3. Remove from oven and let cool.

CINNIE BISCUIT BUNNS

Recipe: (Makes 9 jumbo biscuits bunns)

INGREDIENTS:

1 c. warm milk

2 eggs, room temperature

1/3 c. margarine, melted

4 1/2 c. flour

1 tsp. salt

1/2 c. granulated sugar

2 1/2 tsp. yeast

Cream cheese icing:

8 oz. Cream cheese

1/4 c. butter

1 1/2 c. powdered sugar

1/2 tsp vanilla

DIRECTIONS:

1. In a stand mixer, add warm milk, yeast. Allow yeast to bloom. Feed with 1/4 cup sugar and 1 tsp salt. Reserving 1/4 sugar.

2. Once bloomed, add room temperature eggs, melted margarine, flour and reserved sugar.

3. Put dough hook on stand mixer, kneed on medium for 10 minutes. If you don't have a stand mixer, turn onto floured surface and kneed for 13 minutes. Cover in a greased bowl and let rise for 1 hour.

4. While dough rises. Mix 1/2 cup softened butter with 2 tbsp.brown sugar and 2 tbsp.cinnamon. Combine room temperature cream cheese with 1/4 c. softened butter, vanilla and powdered sugar for icing.

5. Roll out dough on floured surface and spread cinnamon sugar mixture over dough. On one side begin rolling dough up to make large roll.

6. Cut 9 equal rolls and place into greased (butter) 9x13 pan. Cover with towel, let rise 45 minutes.

7. Preheat oven 400°, bake for 15 minutes. Remove from oven and spoon icing over rolls and spread evenly.

Fudge Sandwich

Recipe (Makes 16-18)

INGREDIENTS:

Fudge cookie

1 1/4 c. softened butter

2 c. sugar

2 c. flour

3/4 c. cocoa powder

2 eggs

1 tsp. vanilla

1 tsp. baking soda

Filling

1/2 c. shortening

1/2 c. softened butter

1/4 c. cocoa powder

3 c. powdered sugar

1 tsp. vanilla

DIRECTIONS:

1. Using a stand or hand mixer, place all ingredient for fudge cookie in large bowl. Mix until well combined.

2. Preheat oven to 350°, line cookie sheet with parchment, using a 1 1/2 cookie scoop place out cookies approximately 2 inches apart. Bake at 350° for 8 minutes.

3. Place filling ingredients in medium bowl and mix until well combined.

4. Remove cookies from tray, allow to cool completely.

5. Place filling in pipping bag or storage bag and using scissors cut corner to make a pipping bag. Pipe filling onto one cookie side and top with another cookie. Repeat.

OATMEAL CREME SANDWICH

Recipe: (Makes 12-15)

INGREDIENTS:

1 1/3 c. butter

3 tbsp. shortening

3/4 c. light brown sugar

1/2 c. granulated sugar

1 tsp. molasses

1 tsp. vanilla

2 eggs

1 1/2 c. flour

1 tsp. baking soda

1/8 tsp. cinnamon

Filling:

14 oz. marshmallow creme

1 c. shortening

2/3 c. powdered sugar

1 tsp vanilla

DIRECTIONS:

1. Using a stand or hand mixer, place all ingredient for oatmeal cookie in large bowl. Mix until well combined.

2. Preheat oven to 330º, line cookie sheet with parchment, using a 1 1/2 cookie scoop place out cookies approximately 2 inches apart. Bake at 330º for 8 minutes.

3. Place filling ingredients in medium bowl and mix until well combined.

4. Remove cookies from tray, allow to cool completely.

5. Place filling in pipping bag or storage bag and using scissors cut corner to make a pipping bag. Pipe filling onto one cookie side and top with another cookie. Repeat.

Pecan Pie

Recipe: (Makes one 9 inch pie)

INGREDIENTS:

1 c. sugar

3/4 c. light corn syrup

3/4 c. dark corn syrup

4 eggs

1/4 c. butter

1 1/2 tsp. vanilla

1 1/2 c. pecans, halved

1 pre-made pie shell, or your favorite pie crust recipe

DIRECTIONS:

1. In a sauce pan, boil and whisk together until well combined, sugar and corn syrups. Boil for 2-3 minutes. Remove from heat and cool.

2. In a large bowl, beat eggs. Slowly pour syrup into eggs while whisking.

3. Stir in butter, pecans, and vanilla.

4. Pour into pie shell, I use a store bought one to save time but you can use your favorite pie crust recipe.

5. Preheat oven to 350°. Bake for 45-60 minutes or until set.

Tiramisu

Recipe: (Makes a 8x8 pan)

INGREDIENTS:

6 large egg yolks

1 c. sugar

1 1/4 c. mascarpone cheese, room temperature

1 3/4 c. heavy cream

Savoiardi Lady Fingers

Droste cocoa, or other cocoa powder

2 c. espresso, instant or brewed

Optional:

Marsala wine

Rum

DIRECTIONS:

1. In a double boiler, add 6 egg yolks and 1 cup of the sugar, whisking constantly until well combined and smooth.

2. Remove from heat and let cool, approximately 15-20 minutes. Fold in 1 1/4 cup room temperature mascarpone.

3. While egg mascarpone mixture is cooling to room temperature, beat heavy whipping cream until still peaks form. After peaks form fold in to egg mascarpone mixture until just combined. Do not mix heavily, should be light and airy.

4. Place 2 cups of espresso, Marsala and rum if you choose too, in a cookie sheet. Take Savoiardi lady fingers and quickly press into liquids both sides. Begin lining into 8x8 pan.

5. Layer lady fingers, mascarpone mixture, then lady fingers and so on until you reach top of the 8x8 pan. Last layer should be mascarpone and flush with top of pan.

6. Dust top of pan with Droste cocoa.

SCONES

Recipe: (Makes 6 triangle)

INGREDIENTS:

2 c. flour

4 tsp. baking powder

1/3 c. sugar

4 tbsp. butter

2 tbsp. shortening

3/4 c. heavy whipping cream

1 egg

Optional ingredients:

Fresh fruit

Chocolate chips

Nuts

Herbs and cheese (omit sugar)

Spices

DIRECTIONS:

1. Combine butter, shortening, and flour by hand or with a fork or pastry blender. Until crumbly texture.

2. With a wooden spoon combine remaining ingredient into flour mixture.

3. Turn dough onto floured surface, shape into 9 inch disc. Cut into 6 equal triangles. Place on parchment lined cookie sheet.

4. Preheat oven to 425°, bake scones for 15 minutes. Remove and let cool.

5. Serve with butter, jams and jellies, honey, or your favorite spreads.

ARTISAN BREAD

Recipe: (Makes 1 round loaf)

INGREDIENTS:

3 c. all purpose white unbleached or bread flour

1 tsp. salt

1/2 tsp. yeast

1 1/2 c. warm water (110°F)

Biscuit's notes:

Hair optional. Great with high quality catnip.

Additional options:

Add fresh herbs

Add Kalamata olives

Add cheese

DIRECTIONS:

1. In a medium bowl combine, yeast and water. Let froth about 5 minutes.

2. Mix in flour and salt until forms into a ball. Cover bowl with plastic wrap and let sit 8-24 hours.

3. Uncover dough and turn onto a well floured surface and let rest 30 minutes.

4. Preheat oven to 450°. Preheat dish in oven. Cut with a sharp knife an "X" into top of dough. Cover dough with foil, bake for 30 minutes. Remove foil and bake an additional 10-15 minutes until browned.

Cheddar Biscuits

Recipe: (Makes 15)

INGREDIENTS:

Biscuits

2 c. flour

1 tbsp. baking powder

2 tsp. garlic powder

1/2 tsp. Kosher salt

1 c. buttermilk

1/2 c. butter, melted

1 1/2 c. shredded sharp cheddar

Topping

3 tbsp. butter, melted

1 tbsp. dried parsley

1/2 tsp. garlic powder

DIRECTIONS:

1. Combine all biscuit ingredients, mix by hand until well combined.

2. Using a 2 inch scoop, portion out onto a parchment lined cookie sheet.

3. Preheat oven to 450°, place cookie sheet on middle rack. Back for 10-12 minutes, or until golden brown.

4. Combine melted butter, parsley and garlic. After removing biscuits from oven, brush topping over biscuits.

POPOVERS

<u>Recipe</u> : (Makes 12-15)

INGREDIENTS:

4 eggs, room temperature

1 1/2 c. milk

3/4 tsp. salt

1 1/2 c. flour

3 tbsp. butter, melted

Optional adds:

Cheese

Herbs

Catnip

DIRECTIONS:

1. Using a stand or hand mixer, place all ingredients in a large bowl and combine until there are no lumps. Must be smooth dough.

2. Preheat oven to 450°. Grease a muffin tin and fill each 3/4 of the way full. Bake at 450° for 20 minutes. Reduce oven to 350°, bake an additional 10-15 minutes. **DO NOT OPEN OVEN DOOR DURING BAKING.**

CHOCOLATE DIPPED MACAROONS

Recipe: (Makes 2 dozen)

INGREDIENTS:

1/3 c. butter

3 oz. cream cheese

3/4 c. granulated sugar

1 egg yolk

2 tsp. vanilla

1 1/4 c. flour

2 tsp. baking powder

1/4 tsp. salt

4 c. coconut, shredded and sweetened

8 oz bag of your favorite chocolate

DIRECTIONS:

1. Using a hand or stand mixer, beat butter, cream cheese, and sugar until light and fluffy. Add egg yolk and vanilla.

2. Combine flour and baking powder in a separate bowl, fold in by hand 3 cups of shredded coconut.

3. Combine cream cheese mixture and coconut mixture until well combined. Cover and chill for 1 hour.

4. Shape into 1 inch balls, roll in remaining coconut.

5. Preheat oven to 350º, place balls on parchment lined cookie sheet, bake at 350º for 10 minutes.

6. Microwave chocolate, in a microwave safe bowl. 30 seconds at a time mixing in-between each 30 second interval.

7. Dip cooled macaroons in chocolate and place on parchment lined cookie sheet let chocolate set.

PEPERNOTEN

Recipe: (Makes a stocking full)

INGREDIENTS:

1/2 c. butter

1/2 c. brown sugar

2 tsp. Speculaas

1 1/4 c. flour

2 tbsp. milk

Speculaas

Speculaas (Equal parts no matter the measurement, depending on how much you need, use ground spices)

Cinnamon 8

Nutmeg 2

Clove 2

White pepper 1

Ginger 1

Cardamom 1

DIRECTIONS:

1. Combine al ingredients in a stand mixer, if you don't have a stand mixer, using a hand mixer will do.

2. Remove dough from bowl and roll into 1/2 inch logs. Cut log into even nuggets.

3. Place nuggets on parchment lined cookie sheet. Preheat oven to 350°. Place cookie sheet on middle rack for 8-10 minutes.

4. Remove from oven, let cool 5-10 minutes. Remove from cookies sheet. Allow to cool completely.

Pumpkin Donut Holes

Recipe: (Makes about 15)

INGREDIENTS:

2 c. flour

3/4 c. sugar

1 1/4 c. pumpkin puree

1 egg

2 tbsp. butter, melted

2 tsp. baking powder

2 tsp. pumpkin spice

1 tsp. salt

Oil for frying

Speculaas (Equal parts no matter the measurement depending on how much you need, use ground spices)

Cinnamon 8

Nutmeg 2

Clove 2

White pepper 1

Ginger 1

Cardamom 1

DIRECTIONS:

1. Combine all ingredients into large bowl and mix until well combined.

2. Heat oil in a stock pot, oil should be 375°, use an oil/candy thermometer. Drop 1 1/2 cookie scoop sized balls of dough into oil. When dough floats, pull from oil and drain on paper towel.

3. Allow to cool, roll in speculaas.

From our family to yours, thank you so much for your support. We are honored by your contribution in our endeavors.

Meow, meow, meow. Meeeow, mew, mew, mew. Meow.

Biscuit, Phil & Stephanie

Made in the USA
Coppell, TX
22 October 2020

40045789R00029